Children's
550.78
VanCleave
11/17 $35

JANICE VANCLEAVE'S
WILD, WACKY, AND WEIRD
SCIENCE EXPERIMENTS

EVEN MORE OF JANICE VANCLEAVE'S
WILD, WACKY, AND WEIRD
EARTH SCIENCE
EXPERIMENTS

Illustrations by
Jim Carroll

rosen publishing's
rosen
central®

New York

This edition published in 2018 by
The Rosen Publishing Group, Inc.
29 East 21st Street
New York, NY 10010

Library of Congress Cataloging-in-Publication Data

Names: VanCleave, Janice Pratt.
Title: Even more of Janice VanCleave's wild, wacky, and weird earth science experiments / Janice VanCleave.
Description: New York : Rosen Publishing, 2018. | Series: Janice VanCleave's wild, wacky, and weird science experiments | Audience: Grades 5-8. | Includes bibliographical references and index.
Identifiers: LCCN 2017001882 | ISBN 9781499466898 (library-bound) | ISBN 9781499466942 (pbk.) | ISBN 9781499466805 (6-pack)
Subjects: LCSH: Earth sciences—Experiments—Juvenile literature. | Science projects—Juvenile literature.
Classification: LCC QE29 .V3627 2018 | DDC 550.78—dc23
LC record available at https://lccn.loc.gov/2017001882

Manufactured in China

Illustrations by Jim Carroll

Experiments first published in *Janice VanCleave's 200 Gooey, Slippery, Slimy, Weird and Fun Experiments* by John Wiley & Sons, Inc. copyright © 1992 Janice VanCleave

CONTENTS

INTRODUCTION

Earth science is the study of Earth. Geology is one main area of earth science that deals with the study of our physical planet. But oceanography, meteorology, and astronomy are also branches of earth science.

The people who decide to work in the field of earth science have a variety of career paths to choose from. Some work in laboratories. Others work outdoors and study soil, fossils, volcanos, and earthquakes. All of these people have something in common: They are constantly asking questions to learn even more about our planet.

This book is a collection of science experiments about earth science. How does rain affect topsoil? Does freezing water cause rock movement? How much pressure does air have? You will find the answers to these and many other questions by doing the experiments in this book.

HOW TO USE THIS BOOK

You will be rewarded with successful experiments if you read each experiment carefully, follow the steps in order, and do not substitute materials. The following sections are included for all the experiments.

» **PURPOSE:** *The basic goals for the experiment.*

» **MATERIALS:** *A list of supplies you will need.* You will experience less frustration and more fun if you gather all the necessary materials for the experiments before you begin. You lose your train of thought when you have to stop and search for supplies.

» **PROCEDURE:** *Step-by-step instructions on how to perform the experiment.* Follow each step very carefully, never skip steps, and do not add your own. Safety is of the utmost importance, and by reading the experiment before starting, then following the instructions exactly, you can feel confident that no unexpected results will occur. Ask an adult to help you when you are working with anything sharp or hot. If adult supervision is required, it will be noted in the experiment.

» **RESULTS:** *An explanation stating exactly what is expected to happen.* This is an immediate learning tool. If the expected results are achieved, you will know that you did the experiment correctly. If your results are not the same as described in the experiment, carefully read the instructions and start over from the first step.

» **WHY?** *An explanation of why the results were achieved.*

INTRODUCTION

THE SCIENTIFIC METHOD

Scientists identify a problem or observe an event. Then they seek solutions or explanations through research and experimentation. By doing the experiments in this book, you will learn to follow experimental steps and make observations. You will also learn many scientific principles that have to do with earth science.

In the process, the things you see or learn may lead you to new questions. For example, perhaps you have completed the experiment that investigates whether water pressure is affected by volume. Now you wonder whether water pressure is affected by temperature. That's great! All scientists are curious and ask new questions about what they learn. When you design a new experiment, it is a good idea to follow the scientific method.

1. Ask a question.

2. Do some research about your question. What do you already know?

3. Come up with a hypothesis, or a possible answer to your question.

4. Design an experiment to test your hypothesis. Make sure the experiment is repeatable.

5. Collect the data and make observations.

6. Analyze your results.

7. Reach a conclusion. Did your results support your hypothesis?

Many times the experiment leads to more questions and a new experiment.

Always remember that when devising your own science experiment, have a knowledgeable adult review it with you before trying it out. Ask them to supervise it as well.

NEEDLES

PURPOSE To demonstrate how crystals form.

MATERIALS black construction paper
scissors
lid from a large jar
measuring cup, 1 cup (250 ml)
Epsom salt
measuring spoon, tablespoon (15 ml)

PROCEDURE

1. Cut a circle from the black paper that will fit inside the lid. Place the paper in the lid.

2. Fill the measuring cup with water (250 ml).

3. Add 4 tablespoons (60 ml) of Epsom salt to the water and stir.

4. Pour a very thin layer of the mixture into the lid.

5. Allow the lid to stand undisturbed for one day.

RESULTS Long needle-shaped crystals form on the black paper.

WHY? The Epsom salt molecules move closer together as the water slowly evaporates from the solution. The salt molecules begin to line up in an orderly pattern and form long needle-shaped crystals. The salt molecules stack together like building blocks, and the shape of the molecules determines the resulting shape of the crystal.

8

BUBBLES

PURPOSE To demonstrate a positive test for limestone.

MATERIALS 3 seashells
vinegar
glass

PROCEDURE

1. Fill a glass 1/4 full with vinegar.

2. Add the seashells.

RESULTS Bubbles start rising from the seashells.

WHY? Vinegar is an acid and seashells are made of limestone, a mineral. Limestone chemically changes into new substances when in contact with an acid. One of the new substances formed is carbon dioxide gas, and it is the bubbles of this gas that are seen rising in the glass of vinegar. Acid can be used to test for the presence of limestone in rocks. If limestone is present in a rock, bubbles form when an acid touches the rock.

CRUNCH

PURPOSE To demonstrate the formation of metamorphic rocks.

MATERIALS 20 flat toothpicks
book
table

PROCEDURE

1. Snap the toothpicks in half, but leave them connected.

2. Pile the toothpicks on a table.

3. Place the book on top of the toothpick pile and press down.

4. Remove the book.

RESULTS The toothpicks are pressed into flat layers.

WHY? The toothpicks flatten into layers under the pressure of the book. In nature, the weight of rocks at the surface pushes down on rock and dirt beneath, forcing them to flatten into layers. Rocks formed by great pressure are called metamorphic rock.

SEDIMENTARY SANDWICH

PURPOSE To demonstrate a sedimentary rock formation.

MATERIALS 2 slices of bread   knife, for spreading
peanut butter   plate
jelly

PROCEDURE

Note: Do this activity before lunch, but do NOT do this activity if you or your helpers have a peanut allergy.

1. Lay one slice of bread on a plate.

2. Use the knife to spread a layer of peanut butter on the slice of bread.

3. Add a layer of jelly on top of the peanut butter layer.

4. Place the second slice of bread on top of the jelly layer.

5. Eat the sandwich. *Caution*: Never taste anything in a laboratory setting unless you are sure that there are no harmful chemicals or materials. This experiment is safe.

RESULTS A sandwich with a series of layers has been constructed.

WHY? Sedimentary rocks are formed from loose particles that have been carried from one place to another and redeposited. These rocks usually are deposited in a series of layers similar to the layers in the sandwich. Each layer can be distinguished by differences in color, texture, and composition. The oldest layer and lowest bed is deposited first and the youngest layer is at the top. The layers over a period of time become compacted and cemented together to form solid rock structures.

Sedimentary Sandwich

LINEUP

PURPOSE To demonstrate that some minerals have a definite cleavage line.

MATERIALS paper towels

PROCEDURE

1. Try to rip a single sheet of a paper towel from top to bottom.

2. Turn another sheet of paper towel and try to tear it from side to side.

RESULTS The paper will tear easily in one direction but not in the other.

WHY? Paper towels are made on a wire screen, creating a straight line in one direction. Pulling on the paper attacks the weakest point. The parallel lines on the paper made by the wire screen are thinner than the rest of the paper, and thus the paper rips easily down one of these lines. Jagged and irregular tears result when the paper is pulled in the opposite direction. This is like cutting minerals, such as diamonds, along cleavage lines. The mineral splits smoothly and easily along the lines where the molecules line up, but it can smash into irregular pieces if hit across the cleavage line.

Even More of Janice VanCleave's Wild, Wacky, and Weird Earth Science Experiments

FOLDS

PURPOSE To demonstrate how compressional forces affect crustal movement.

MATERIALS 4 paper towels
glass of water

PROCEDURE

1. Stack the paper towels on a table.

2. Fold the stack of paper in half.

3. Wet the paper with water.

4. Place your hands on the edges of the wet paper.

5. Slowly push the sides of the paper toward the center.

RESULTS The paper has many folds.

WHY? Your hands push the sides of the paper toward the center. Parts of the paper fold over so that it fits into the smaller space provided. When forces from opposite directions push against sections of Earth's crust, the compressed land is squeezed into new shapes called folds. The upper surface of this folded land has a wavelike appearance.

Folds

EASY OVER?

PURPOSE To demonstrate the pressure required to fold Earth's crust.

MATERIALS 1 sheet of newspaper

PROCEDURE

1. Fold the paper in half.

2. Continue to fold the paper as many times as you can.

RESULTS The paper becomes more difficult to fold. After the sixth or seventh folding, you will be unable to bend the paper.

WHY? With each folding, the amount of paper doubles. After seven foldings, there are 128 sheets. Earth's crust, like the paper, requires a small amount of pressure to fold thin, lighter layers on the surface. Tremendous amounts of pressure are required to fold over large, denser sections of land.

Easy Over?

SLOWER

PURPOSE To determine why seismic waves move slowly through sand.

MATERIALS paper towel
paper core from roll of paper towels
uncooked rice
rubber band

PROCEDURE

1. Cover the end of the paper core with one paper towel.

2. Secure the paper towel to the tube with the rubber band.

3. Fill the tube with rice.

4. Use your fingers to push down on the rice. Try to push the rice down and out through the paper towel.

RESULTS The rice is not pushed through the bottom of the tube. The rice moves very little.

WHY? Sand particles, like the rice, move in all directions when pushed. Vibrations from seismic waves move more slowly through sand because the forward energy of the wave moves in different directions as the sand particles move outward in all directions.

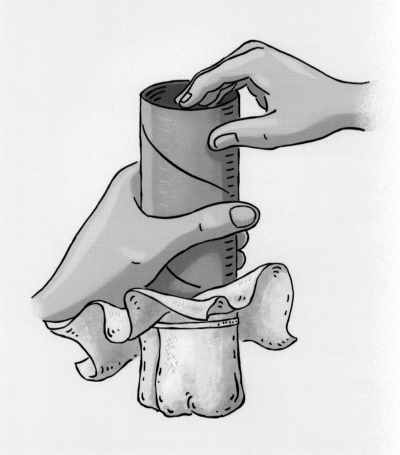

Slower

WAVES

PURPOSE To determine the effect of different materials on the speed of p-waves (primary waves) produced by earthquakes.

MATERIALS ruler
string
scissors
masking tape
table

PROCEDURE

1. Measure and cut a 30-in. (76-cm) length of string.

2. Tape one end of the string to a table.

3. Hold the free end of the string and stretch the string.

4. Strum the stretched string with your finger. Listen.

5. Wrap the end of the string around your index finger.

6. Place the tip of your finger in your ear.

7. Strum the stretched string with your fingers.

RESULTS The sound is much louder when you put your finger in your ear.

WHY? The vibrations from the string travel faster through the string attached to a solid than through the air. Primary waves, p-waves, are the first recorded vibrations from an earthquake. These waves travel as compression waves similar to sound waves. P-waves move faster when traveling through dense materials—materials that have their molecules close together. The speed of p-waves gives clues to the density of the materials through which they travel.

RIPPLES

PURPOSE To demonstrate how seismic waves give clues to the content of Earth's interior.

MATERIALS bowl, 2 qt. (2 liter)
glass soft-drink bottle
pencil

PROCEDURE

1. Fill the bowl about halfway with water.

2. Set the bottle in the center of the bowl of water.

3. Tap the surface of the water several times near the side of the bowl with a pencil.

RESULTS Waves ripple out from where the pencil touches the water. The waves hit the bottle and most are reflected back toward the pencil.

WHY? The pencil vibrates the water, sending out waves of energy, but the waves are not able to move through the bottle. S-waves are secondary waves that arrive after the faster primary waves (p-waves). Both these waves are produced by earthquakes. S-waves are slower and have less energy than p-waves. These less energetic waves can move through solids but not through liquids. The s-waves move through the solid part of Earth but, like the water waves hitting the bottle, are reflected back by Earth's liquid core. P-waves travel through the center of Earth, but s-waves are reflected back, which indicates that the inner part of Earth is in liquid form.

PURPOSE To demonstrate the effect of rain on hills with and without ground cover.

MATERIALS 3 large shallow baking pans
table
modeling clay
ruler
2 cups of soil
quart (liter) bowl filled with a mixture of leaves, grass, and small twigs
1 drinking glass

PROCEDURE

1. Place a shallow baking pan on a table.

2. Use clay to position two pans so that they are raised about 2 in. (5 cm) at one end, with their other ends resting inside the pan on the table as in the diagram.

3. Spread one cup of soil across the top section of the pans.

4. Cover the soil on one of the pans with the mixture of grass, leaves, and small twigs.

5. Hold a tilted glass full of water about 6 in. (15 cm) above the uncovered soil and allow the water to slowly pour onto the soil.

6. Repeat the procedure on the covered soil.

7. Compare the amount of soil collected at the bottom of each elevated pan.

RESULTS More soil washes away from the uncovered soil.

WHY? Unprotected soil dissolves in the flowing water and moves down the pan. In nature, leaves, grass, and small twigs provide a protective covering. This covering holds the soil in place and soaks up water that might wash away the soil. Plants that grow in the soil provide even more protection because their roots help hold the soil in place. The washing away of soil is called erosion.

Rock Eater

PURPOSE To demonstrate the effect of acid on statues.

MATERIALS chalk
vinegar
glass

PROCEDURE

1. Fill a glass 1/4 full with vinegar.

2. Add a piece of chalk to the glass.

RESULTS Bubbles start rising from the chalk. Small pieces start to break off, and finally the chalk totally breaks apart.

WHY? Vinegar is an acid and acids slowly react chemically with the chalk. The piece of chalk is made of limestone, a mineral that quickly changes into new substances when touched by an acid. One of the new substances is the gas seen rising in the vinegar, which is carbon dioxide gas. Acids affect all minerals, but the change is usually slow. The slow deterioration of statues and building fronts is due to the weak acid rain that falls on the statue. If the stone is limestone or has limestone in it, the deterioration is more rapid. Some stones are more resistant to the acid attack.

Rock Eater

RUNOFF

PURPOSE To demonstrate how rain affects topsoil.

MATERIALS soil
red powdered tempera paint
measuring spoon, teaspoon (5 ml)
stirring spoon
funnel
wide-mouthed jar, 1 qt. (1 liter)
coffee filter paper
measuring cup, 1 cup (250 ml)

PROCEDURE

1. Add ¼ teaspoon (1.25 ml) of red tempera paint to ¼ cup (75 ml) of soil. Mix thoroughly.

2. Set the funnel in the jar.

3. Place the coffee filter inside the funnel.

4. Pour the colored soil into the paper filter.

5. Add ¼ cup (75 ml) of water to the funnel.

6. Observe the water dripping into the jar.

7. Pour this water out of the jar and add another ¼ cup (75 ml) of water to the funnel.

RESULTS The liquid dripping out of the funnel is red.

WHY? The red paint represents nutrients in topsoil that are soluble in water. Nutrients dissolve in rainwater and feed the plants growing in the soil. If the rain is too heavy, the water runs across the land, taking the dissolved nutrients with it. Excessive rains can leave the topsoil lacking in necessary nutrients.

FLY AWAY

PURPOSE To determine how moisture affects land erosion.

MATERIALS paper hole punch
shallow baking pan
sheet of paper
bowl of water

PROCEDURE

1. Cut about fifty paper circles from the paper with the paper hole punch.

2. Place the paper circles in the pan at one end.

3. Blow across the paper circles.

4. Wet your fingers in the bowl of water and sprinkle the water over the paper circles. You want the paper to be damp.

5. Blow across the paper circles again.

RESULTS The dry paper particles easily move to the opposite end of the pan and some fly out of the pan. The wet paper does not move easily.

WHY? Loose, lightweight particles can be picked up by the wind and carried for long distances. Flyaway surface particles that are easily supported by the wind are commonly found in deserts and along shorelines. The damp paper circles stick together and are too heavy for your breath to lift. Damp land areas and those covered by vegetation are not as easily eroded by the wind because, like the damp paper, the materials are too heavy to be lifted by the wind.

CRACK-UP

PURPOSE To determine if freezing water causes rock movement.

MATERIALS drinking straw
modeling clay
glass of water
freezer

PROCEDURE

1. Place one end of the straw into the glass of water.

2. Fill the straw by sucking the water into it.

3. Hold your tongue over one end to prevent the water from escaping while you insert a clay plug into the open end of the straw.

4. Remove your tongue and plug the end with clay.

5. Lay the straw in the freezer for three hours.

6. Remove the straw and observe the ends.

RESULTS One of the clay plugs has been pushed out of the straw and a column of ice is extending past the end of the straw.

WHY? Water, unlike most substances, expands when it freezes. When water gets into cracks in and around rocks, it can actually move or break the rock when it freezes. The expansion of the freezing water is enough to push apart weak points in the rocks. This is the main cause of potholes in the streets.

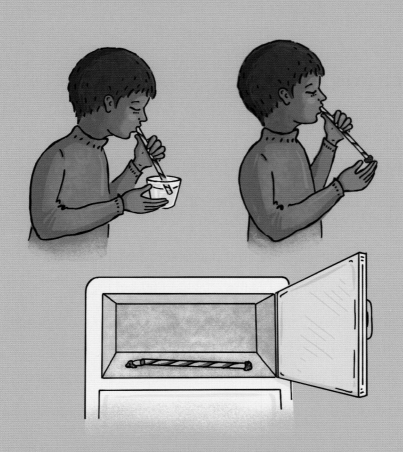

Crack-Up

Holding

PURPOSE To determine how much pressure air has.

MATERIALS 1 yardstick (meter stick)
table
1 sheet of newspaper

PROCEDURE

1. Place the measuring stick on a table so that half of the stick extends over the edge of the table.

2. Fold a sheet of newspaper in half four times.

3. Place the folded paper over the end of the measuring stick that is lying on the table.

4. With your index finger, tap the end of the measuring stick.

5. Observe the movement of the stick and folded paper.

6. Unfold the sheet of newspaper and spread it over the measuring stick so that the paper lies flat along the table's edge.

7. Tap the end of the measuring stick with the same force as before.

8. Again observe the movement of the newspaper and measuring stick.

RESULTS The newspaper is more difficult to lift when spread out than when folded.

WHY? The weight of the folded and flat newspaper is the same. It is the pressure of the air on the paper that prevents it from rising. More than

250 miles (156 km) of air extending upward from the top of the paper presses the paper against the table. This column of air above the paper pushes down with a force of 15 lb. per square inch (1 kilogram per square centimeter). The average force on the surface of the folded paper is 578 lb. (263 kg). Laying the paper flat produces a surface about 16 times as large, and thus the pressure of the air is 16 times as great, or 9,248 lbs. (4,208 kg).

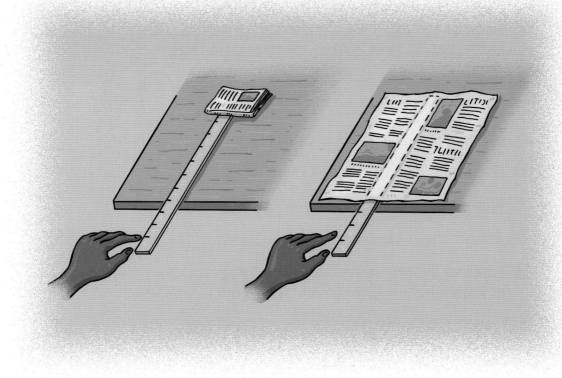

RHYTHMIC

PURPOSE To demonstrate how a gentle breeze can move heavy objects.

MATERIALS string wide-tipped marking pen
scissors masking tape
ruler table

PROCEDURE

1. Cut a piece of string about 18 in. (45 cm) long.

2. Tie one end of the string to the top of the marking pen.

3. Tape the free end of the string to the top edge of a table with the pen hanging about 12 in. (30 cm) below the table's top.

4. Kneel on the floor with the suspended pen about 12 in. (30 cm) in front of your face.

5. Blow as hard as possible toward the pen.

6. Observe the height the pen moves.

7. Stop the pen from moving.

8. Blow on the pen with a small puff of breath.

9. Wait until the moving pen begins its swing away from your face and hit it with a small puff of breath. Do this ten times.

10. Again observe the height the pen moves.

RESULTS The pen moves to a greater height when hit with small puffs of breath at the beginning of its swing than with one hard blast of breath.

WHY? The amplitude (height) of any swinging object can be greatly increased by rhythmically applying a gentle push. Every object has a natural vibration (rate at which it can move back and forth). Applying a force at the same time an object starts its vibration is similar to "pumping" a playground swing at just the right time in each cycle; both increase the amplitude of motion.

SPRAYER

PURPOSE To demonstrate how air pressure can be used to produce a spraying fountain.

MATERIALS 1 common nail, #8 x 3.5 in.
hammer
adult helper
ruler
2 pint (500 ml) jars, one with a lid

2 straws
modeling clay
green food coloring
baking dish

PROCEDURE

1. Ask an adult to use the hammer and nail to make two holes in the lid.

2. Push one straw through a hole so that 2 in. (5 cm) extends above the lid. (Straw A in the diagram.)

3. Push the second straw through the other hole in the lid so that about 2 in. (5 cm) extends inside the lid. (Straw B in the diagram.)

4. Use small pieces of modeling clay to seal the opening between the straws and the lid.

5. Fill one jar halfway with water and screw on the lid.

6. Fill the second jar with water and add enough food coloring to turn it dark green.

7. Set the jar of colored water in a baking dish.

8. Turn the jar with the straws through the lid upside down with the shortest straw beneath the colored water in the jar.

9. Observe the ends of the two straws.

RESULTS Colored water rises and sprays out of straw A inside the closed jar. Water from the closed jar runs out of straw B and into the open baking dish.

WHY? Gravity (the downward pull toward the center of Earth) pulls the water out of the closed jar and down through straw B. As the water leaves, the air in the jar spreads out, and the air pressure inside the closed jar is reduced. The air pressure outside the closed jar is now greater than the air pressure inside the jar. The air pushing down on the colored water forces the water up and out of straw A. The result is a spraying fountain inside the closed jar.

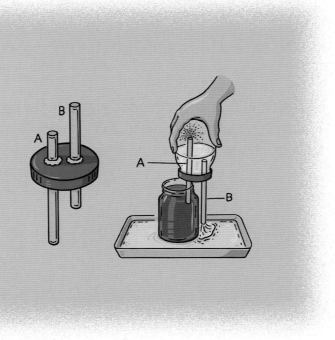

Sprayer

SPACEY

PURPOSE To demonstrate that air takes up space.

MATERIALS bowl, 2 qt. (2 liter)
small cork
clear drinking glass

PROCEDURE

1. Fill the bowl halfway with water.

2. Float the cork on the water's surface.

3. Hold the glass above the floating cork.

4. Press the open mouth of the glass down into the water.

RESULTS The surface of the water with the floating cork is pushed down.

WHY? The pocket of air inside the glass prevents the water from entering the glass, so the water with the floating cork is forced down below the level of the water outside the glass.

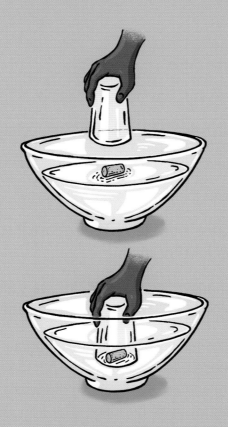

STRAW DRILL

PURPOSE To demonstrate the strength of air.

MATERIALS 1 raw potato

2 plastic drinking straws

PROCEDURE

1. Place the potato on a table.

2. Hold the straw at the top, leaving the top open.

3. Raise the straw about 4 in. (10 cm) above the potato.

4. Quickly and with force stick the end of the straw into the potato.

5. Hold your thumb over the top of the second straw.

6. Again raise the straw about 4 in. (10 cm) above the potato, and with force stick the straw into the potato.

RESULTS The open-ended straw bends, and very little of the straw enters the potato. The closed straw cuts deeply into the potato.

WHY? Air is composed mainly of the gases nitrogen, oxygen, and carbon dioxide. These gases are invisible, but the results of their pressure can be observed. Fast-moving air (wind) can apply enough pressure to destroy large buildings. The trapped air inside the straw makes the straw strong enough to break through the skin of the potato. The push of the air against the inside of the straw prevents it from bending. The pressure of the air increases as the plug of potato enters and compresses the air.

Straw

Potato

DRIPPY

PURPOSE To demonstrate 100 percent humidity.

MATERIALS baking pan
table
sponge
eyedropper

PROCEDURE

1. Fill the baking pan with water and set the pan on a table.

2. Place the sponge on a table.

3. Fill the eyedropper with water from the baking pan.

4. Squeeze one drop of water from the eyedropper onto the sponge.

5. Pick the sponge up with your hands and observe the bottom of the sponge.

6. Place the sponge in the pan of water. Turn the sponge over in the water a couple of times.

7. Again pick the sponge up with your hands, holding it above the pan of water.

8. Observe the bottom of the sponge.

RESULTS With one drop of water, the bottom of the sponge remains dry. Water drips out of the sponge after it is allowed to soak in the water.

WHY? Air can be compared with the sponge in that they both can hold water. One drop of water in the sponge made very little difference, but soaking the sponge allowed it to become saturated (completely filled with water). Water dripped out of the sponge when it was unable to hold any more water. Air, like the sponge, can be saturated with water when it is filled to its capacity. Relative humidity is the amount of water in the air compared with its capacity. When the air is saturated, it is said to have a 100 percent humidity.

SPONGE DRIPPING WATER

TRAY OF WATER

EYEDROPPER

UP AND DOWN

PURPOSE To demonstrate how a thermometer works.

MATERIALS outdoor thermometer
cup
ice cube

PROCEDURE

1. Hold the bulb of the thermometer between your fingers.

2. Observe the level of the liquid in the thermometer.

3. Fill the cup with water. Add an ice cube and stir.

4. Place the bulb of the thermometer in the cold water.

5. Observe the level of the liquid in the thermometer.

RESULTS Holding the bulb between your fingers caused the liquid in the thermometer to rise. The liquid lowered in the thermometer column when the bulb was placed in cold water.

WHY? Heat from your fingers increases the temperature of the liquid inside the thermometer. As the liquid is heated, it expands and rises in the thermometer tube. The cold water removes heat from the liquid in the thermometer. As the liquid cools, it contracts and moves down the tube. Outdoor thermometers are used to measure the temperature of air. Any increase or decrease in the heat content of air causes the liquid inside the thermometer to expand or contract, thus indicating the temperature of the surrounding air.

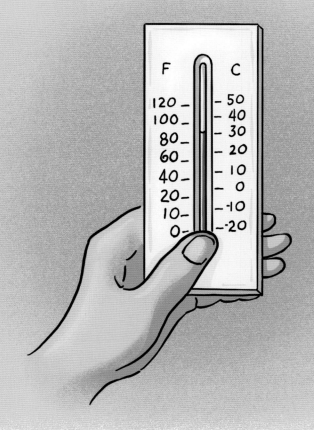

CLOUD WATCHER

PURPOSE To determine wind direction by use of a nephoscope.

MATERIALS paper   compass
               outside table   marking pen
               mirror

PROCEDURE

1. Try this experiment on different days when the sky has separate clumps of moving clouds.

2. Lay a sheet of paper on an outside table.

3. Place a mirror in the center of the paper.

4. Use a compass to determine the direction of north. Mark the direction on the paper with the marking pen.

5. Look into the mirror and watch the image of the clouds as they move cross the mirror.

6. Record the directions that the clouds are coming from.

RESULTS The image of the clouds moves across the mirror.

WHY? The direction and speed of surface winds are changed by obstructions such as trees and buildings. This is why meteorologists and weather forecasters seek information about wind in the upper air. The instrument that you have made is called a nephoscope. It allows you to observe drifting clouds in order to determine the direction of wind in the upper air. Winds are named for the direction they come from. A north wind comes from the north and blows south.

WET AIR

PURPOSE To demonstrate the use of hair in measuring humidity.

MATERIALS   clear tape   marker
straight strand of hair about   pencil
5 in. (12 cm) long   large glass jar
flat toothpick   glue

PROCEDURE

1. Use a small piece of tape to secure one end of the strand of hair to the center of the toothpick.

2. Color the pointed end of the toothpick with the marker.

3. Tape the free end of the hair strand to the center of the pencil.

4. Place the pencil across the mouth of the jar with the toothpick hanging inside the jar. If the toothpick does not hang horizontally, add a drop of glue to the light end to balance the toothpick.

5. Place the jar where it will be undisturbed.

6. Observe the directions that the toothpick points for one week.

RESULTS The toothpick changes direction.

WHY? You have made a hair hygrometer. Hygrometers are instruments used to measure humidity, the amount of water in air. The hair stretches when the humidity increases; with a lower humidity, the hair shrinks. The stretching and shrinking of the hair pulls on the toothpick, causing it to move.

GLOSSARY

AMPLITUDE Height.

EROSION The washing away of soil.

EVAPORATION The process by which a liquid absorbs enough heat to change into a gas.

GRAVITY The downward pull toward the center of Earth.

HUMIDITY The amount of water in air.

HYGROMETER A tool used to measure the amount of water in the air, or humidity.

METAMORPHIC ROCK Rock formed by great pressure.

MOLECULE The smallest particle of a substance; made of one or more atoms.

NATURAL VIBRATION The rate at which an object can move back and forth.

NEPHOSCOPE A tool used to observe moving clouds to determine the direction of wind in the upper air.

NUTRIENT A substance needed for growth and life.

P-WAVES Primary waves; the first recorded vibrations from an earthquake.

RELATIVE HUMIDITY The amount of water in the air compared with its capacity.

SATURATED Completely filled.

SEDIMENTARY ROCK Rock that is formed when loose particles have been carried from one place to another and redeposited, usually in a series of layers.

S-WAVES Secondary waves; waves that are slower than p-waves and have less energy.

FOR MORE INFORMATION

Canadian Federation of Earth Sciences (CFES)
  Department of Earth Sciences
  FSS Hall
  Room 15025
  Ottawa ON K1N 6N5
  Canada
  (902) 697-7425
  Website: http://www.cfes-fcst.ca
  The CFES is a federation of earth science member societies throughout
  Canada. Read about careers, get your earth science questions answered
  by an expert with the Ask a Geoscientist! tool, or use their Earth Links to
  find a multitude of resources about earth science.

National Aeronautics and Space Administration (NASA)
  Ames Earth Science Division
  NASA Headquarters
  300 E. Street SW, Suite 5R30
  Washington, DC 20546
  (202) 358-0001
  Website: http://geo.arc.nasa.gov
  NASA is the premier organization for all things about space and planet
  Earth! Join the NASA Kids' Club, see photos of Earth from space, and
  learn more about earth science research.

National Center for Earth and Space Science Education (NCESSE)
  PO Box 2350
  Ellicott City, MD 21041-2350
  (301) 395-0770
  Website: http://ncesse.org

The NCESSE creates and oversees national programs addressing STEM education, with a focus on earth and space. Check out their links to Family Science Night, contests, experiment programs, and other community events.

The National Geographic Society
1145 17th St. NW
Washington, DC 20036
Museum (202) 857-7700
Website: http://www.nationalgeographic.com
The National Geographic Society has been inspiring people to care about the planet since 1888. It is one of the largest nonprofit scientific and educational institutions in the world. Read their *Kids* magazine, enter the National Geographic Bee, or visit the museum.

National Science Foundation (NSF)
4201 Wilson Boulevard
Arlington, VA 22230
(703) 292-5111
Website: http://www.nsf.gov
The NSF is dedicated to science, engineering, and education. Learn how to be a Citizen Scientist, read about the latest scientific discoveries, and find out about the newest innovations in technology.

The Society for Science and the Public
Student Science
1719 N Street NW
Washington, DC 20036
(800) 552-4412

59

FOR MORE INFORMATION

Website: http://student.societyforscience.org
The Society for Science and the Public presents many science resources, such as science news for students, the latest updates on the Intel Science Talent Search and the Intel International Science and Engineering Fair, and information about cool jobs and doing science.

US Geological Survey (USGS)
12201 Sunrise Valley Drive
Reston, VA 20192
(888) 275-8747
Website: http://www.usgs.gov
The USGS collects, monitors, analyzes, and provides scientific data about natural resource conditions, issues, and problems on Earth. Check out their aerial and satellite images, use their many educational resources, or ask a librarian to help with your earth science questions.

WEBSITES

Because of the changing nature of internet links, Rosen Publishing has developed an online list of websites related to the subject of this book. This site is updated regularly. Please use this link to access the list:

http://www.rosenlinks.com/JVCW/earth

FOR FURTHER READING

Buczynski, Sandy. *Designing a Winning Science Fair Project* (Information Explorer Junior). Ann Arbor, MI: Cherry Lake Publishing, 2014.

Dickmann, Nancy. *Exploring Planet Earth and the Moon* (Spectacular Space Science). New York, NY: Rosen Publishing's Rosen Central, 2016.

Garbe, Suzanne. *Living Earth: Exploring Life on Earth with Science Projects* (Fact Finders: Discover Earth Science). North Mankato, MN: Capstone Press, 2016.

Harris, Tim, ed. *Earth Science* (Science Q&A). New York, NY: Cavendish Square, 2016.

Hyde, Natalie. *Earthquakes, Eruptions, and Other Events that Change Earth* (Earth Processes Close-Up). New York, NY: Crabtree Publishing Co., 2016.

Katirgis, Jane. *Eerie Earthquakes* (Earth's Natural Disasters). New York, NY: Enslow Publishing, Inc., 2016.

Latta, Sara. *All About Earth: Exploring the Planet with Science Projects* (Fact Finders: Discover Earth Science). North Mankato, MN: Capstone Press, 2016.

Lawrence, Ellen. *What's Soil Made Of?* (Down and Dirty: The Secrets of Soil). New York, NY: Bearport Publishing, 2016.

Shea, Therese. *Freaky Weather Stories* (Freaky True Science). New York: Gareth Stevens Publishing, 2016.

Sneideman, Joshua, and Erin Twamley. *Renewable Energy: Discover the Fuel of the Future with 20 Projects* (Build-It-Yourself). White River Junction, VT: Nomad Press, 2016.

Sohn, Emily. *Experiments in Earth Science and Weather with Toys and Everyday Stuff* (First Facts: Fun Science). North Mankato, MN: Capstone Press, 2016.

INDEX

A

acid, 10, 30

air

    pressure, 38–39, 42–43, 46

    saturation, 49, 54–55

    temperature, 50

    volume, 44

C

carbon dioxide, 10, 30, 46

chalk, 30

clouds, 52–53

crystals, 8

D

diamonds, 16

E

Earth

    crustal movement, 18, 20

    gravity, 43

    interior, 26

earthquakes, 24–25, 26

Epsom salt, 8

erosion, 29, 34

evaporation, 8

F

force, 18, 39

G

gravity, 43

H

hair, 54

humidity, 48–49, 54

hygrometer, 54

L

limestone, 10, 30

M

metamorphic rock, 12

minerals, 10, 16, 30

N

nephoscope, 52

P

primary waves (p-waves), 24, 26

R

rain, 28–29, 30, 32–33

rocks

    and erosion, 29, 34

    formation of, 12, 14

    metamorphic, 12

    movement of, 18, 36

    sedimentary, 14

INDEX